The Bat House Builder's Handbook

CONTENTS

You can purchase copies of this handbook or sign up for the North American Bat House Research Project through the BCI catalogue. Call 1-800-538-BATS (2287) or (512) 327-9721.

Putting up a bat house is one of the more rewarding ways to help wildlife. This house is filled with Mexican free-tailed bats, though they typically prefer smaller crevice widths than are shown here.

BAXTER AND CAROL ADAMS

Why Build a Bat House?

AMERICA'S BATS ARE an invaluable natural resource. Yet, due to decades of unwarranted human fear and persecution, bats are in alarming decline. You can help by putting up a bat house. You will benefit from having fewer lawn and garden pests, and you will enjoy learning about bats and sharing your knowledge with friends and neighbors. Few efforts on behalf of wildlife are more fun or rewarding than helping bats.

As primary predators of night-flying insects, bats play a vital role in maintaining the balance of nature. As consumers of vast numbers of pests, they rank among humanity's most valuable allies. A single little brown bat can catch hundreds of mosquitoes in an hour, and a typical colony of 150 big brown bats can protect local farmers from the costly attacks of 18 million rootworms each summer. Cucumber and June beetles, stink bugs, leafhoppers, and cutworm and corn earworm moths—all well-known pests—are just a few of the many insects known to be consumed by these frequent users of bat houses.

Although bat house building may someday contribute greatly even to saving endangered species, our first goal is to preserve America's most abundant bats in sufficient numbers to maintain nature's balance. Their loss contributes to growing demands for toxic pesticides that increasingly threaten our personal and environmental health.

Recent BCI research on bat houses documents substantial success and exciting potential for helping rebuild healthy populations of some of America's most valuable species. More importantly, it shows how slight modifications, often as simple as moving a house only a few feet higher or into slightly more or less sun, can substantially improve the odds of successful occupation by bats.

These results, combined with new knowledge of bat preferences, are very encouraging. However, there is still much we need to learn to consistently attract nursery colonies in a variety of climates. We also have much to learn about how best to meet the needs of individual species.

Participate in the North American Bat House Research Project

INSTALLING BAT HOUSES and making careful observations offers an excellent opportunity to learn more about bat roosting requirements. To encourage experimentation, BCI has established the North American Bat House Research Project. We invite bat house enthusiasts throughout the United States and Canada to make an important contribution to our understanding of bat roosting behavior by participating as active volunteer Research Associates in this long-term project.

Even the most abundant bats of North America are rapidly losing roosting habitat. Although we know that at least nine species are using bat houses, we need more information before we can consistently accommodate even these bats' needs. High priorities include learning more about preferred roost chamber dimensions for individual species and the effects of insulation and solar heating under various climatic conditions.

The amount of time each volunteer needs to commit will range from minimal to as much as you care to devote to the project. From spring to fall, depending on your area, you will be asked to make regular monthly inspections of your bat houses. In addition, it will be critical that you complete and return a simple data report to BCI for each house erected and then a status follow-up at the end of each summer.

Participants will receive complete instructions on how to begin conducting the experiments most needed in their areas along with report forms. The most important data on temperature preferences will result from erecting groups of at least two or three houses, but those who can erect only one house can also contribute valuable information about the incidence of occupancy when single versus multiple roost choices are available. Individuals unable to build their own bat houses may still participate by purchasing them from the BCI catalogue. We strongly encourage those who have unoccupied bat houses to participate by moving them or making other appropriate changes and reporting the results.

Participants will receive special spring and fall reports on bat house research progress; also, they will be able to use this forum to share their experiences and exchange ideas with other project experimenters. Those who successfully attract bats (or who already have done so) and complete and return the data forms, will

Volunteer Research Associates Needed . . .

be eligible to compete for grants to conduct further experiments. In addition, special achievement awards will be made to those who contribute most to new knowledge.

The resources required to mount a national species-specific study of bat roosting needs are truly formidable. Establishing a special project fund by enlisting the participation of contributing volunteers will enable this important work to continue. The project fund supports the costs of phone and mail consultation with participants, data gathering, analysis, and reporting. It will also support small grants and awards to encourage successful participants to expand their research. The North American Bat House Research Project is open to current BCI members and to nonmembers.

Participation as a Research Associate in BCI's North American Bat House Research Project offers a unique opportunity to help your own backyard bats while sharing in the excitement and satisfaction of scientific discovery.

Your participation can yield important information. Please fill out the application included in this handbook and return it to BCI, North American Bat House Research Project, P.O. Box 162603, Austin, Texas 78716.

Designing Better Bat Houses

New research discoveries have greatly enhanced our ability to attract bats . . .

THROUGH THE North American Bat House Research Project, hundreds of new bat houses are tested each year. The designs illustrated on the following pages incorporate the most successful features thus far discovered. The correct bat house for you will depend on available tools and lumber, your skill as a carpenter, your budget, and your expectations. There are also many modifications you can make to your house(s) to adjust for location-specific factors such as climate and the preferences of local species.

Key Criteria for Successful Bat Houses

Design
The most successful bat houses are approximately two feet tall, at least 14 or more inches wide, and have 3- to 6-inch landing areas extending below the entrances. The number of roosting chambers is not critical. Single-chambered houses are often successful when mounted on wooden or stone buildings, which help to buffer temperature fluctuations. Houses with three to four chambers are more likely to provide appropriate ranges of temperature and better accommodate the larger numbers of bats typical of nursery colonies. However, houses with more than six chambers may not absorb adequate solar heat in cool climates.

Our house sizes are a compromise between bat needs and builder convenience. For example, $17^1/_2$-inch widths for nursery houses enable builders to make two houses from a half sheet each of $1/_4$-inch and $1/_2$-inch plywood. This is the minimum amount stores will sell of either of the two required thicknesses and results in the least waste. Widths of up to 24 inches or more would likely be preferred by many bats. Greater heights are not typically necessary, but might be appreciated for their greater thermal gradients.

Roost partitions should be carefully spaced $3/_4$-inch to 1 inch apart—mostly $3/_4$-inch. Some small myotis and pipistrelle bats may prefer roosting crevices between $1/_2$-inch and $3/_4$-inch wide, while larger bats, such as big brown and pallid bats, may possibly prefer 1-inch to $1^1/_4$-inch widths. Partitions and landing areas must be roughened. Wood surfaces can simply be scratched, but are best covered with durable plastic screening ($1/_8$-inch or $1/_4$-inch mesh). We especially recommend plastic screening of the type sold by Internet, Inc. (1-800-328-8456, product numbers XV1670 or XV1170). Screening must be securely stapled down along all exposed edges and should not cover ventilation slots. It is attached to one side of each roost partition as well as to the landing area.

Ventilation slots are critically important in all houses to be used where average high temperatures in July are 85°F or above. They should be $1/_2$-inch wide to reduce entry of light and unwanted guests, such as birds. The front vent should extend from side to side about six inches above the bottom. A vertical vent, $1/_2$-inch wide by six inches long, should be included at each end of the rear chamber of multiple-chamber houses. The vents greatly reduce the odds of overheating on extra hot days and especially contribute to success in moderate or hot climates. They may be unnecessary in exceptionally cool areas.

When nursery houses are mounted in back-to-back pairs (see Figure 2), an additional horizontal vent slot should be provided in the rear—just like the one in front, but $3/_4$-inch rather than $1/_2$-inch wide. This slot allows bats to move from one house to the other without exiting. Such an arrangement provides ideal temperature ranges for nursery colonies.

Construction
Half-inch plywood is ideal for fronts, backs, and roofs, while 1-inch board lumber is best for the sides. Use of $1/_4$-inch plywood for roosting partitions substantially reduces overall bat house weight and enables more roosting space for a given house size. Staples used to attach plastic mesh should not protrude from the far sides of panels and will last longer if they are exterior grade and galvanized. All seams must be caulked, especially around the roof, prior to painting. Latex caulk is easiest to use.

Wood treatment
Bats apparently like dry, non-drafty homes as much as we do, hence the need to carefully caulk and paint bat houses. Providing sufficient warmth without overheating is a key element in attracting bats. All outer sur-

faces and entry areas of bat houses should be painted with at least two coats of exterior latex paint to ensure against moisture, air leaks, and wood deterioration. Available observations demonstrate that bat houses in cool climates need to absorb much more solar heat than those in hot climates. They should be black where average high temperatures in July are 80-85°F or less; dark (such as dark brown, gray, or green) where they are 85-95°F; medium or light where they are 95-100°F; and white where they exceed 100°F. Much depends upon the amount of sun exposure. Darker colors help absorb more heat from less sun.

Sun exposure

When choosing a bat house location, both sun exposure and heat absorption (according to house color) must be carefully considered. Too little sun exposure is the most important known cause of bat house failure, even in relatively hot climates as far south as Florida and Texas. Overheating, though a possibility, can be greatly reduced by use of ventilation slots (see "Design" section) that allow heat to build up above but not below. Ventilated houses allow bats to move vertically to find their preferred temperatures through daily and seasonal cycles, providing a wider margin for error in selecting appropriate sun exposure and color. Bats in nursery colonies like warm houses, ideally where temperature gradients cover at least a 10-15°F range, predominantly between 80° and 100°F, meaning that their roosts require solar heating in all but the hottest climates. The graph in Figure 1 illustrates the impact of solar heating on a black bat house by comparing internal bat house temperature with ambient outside temperature in a house occupied by a nursery colony of little brown bats.

In areas where high temperatures in July average 80°F or less, houses should be dark colored, and should receive at least 10 hours of daily sun; more hours may be better. Even in areas where high temperatures in July average less than 100°F, houses of appropriate color (see "Wood treatment" section) should receive at least six hours of direct daily sun.

When two houses are mounted back-to-back in pairs, attached at the sides, and covered by a tin roof (see Figure 2), solar heat gain is high early and late, but reduced by midday when overheating is most likely. A wide range of temperatures is provided between the house exposed to full sun and the one which is largely shaded by the other, in part because heat transfer is minimized by the fully ventilated area that remains between.

By roughening the backs of both houses and provid-

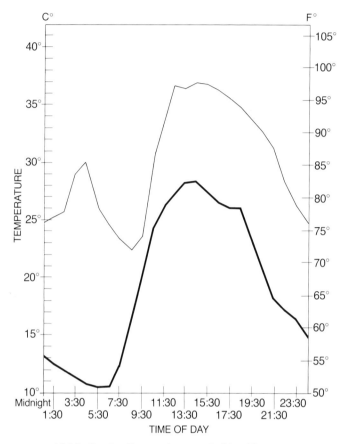

FIGURE 1

This graph compares internal versus external temperatures over a 24-hour cycle at a bat house occupied by a nursery colony of little brown bats in Pennsylvania. Temperatures in roosting crevices remained in the 80-100°F range for 19 hours of the daily cycle, falling below 80° only for five hours in early morning. The house is similar to our nursery design and is vented, covered with black tar paper, and exposed to approximately seven hours of full sun each morning. **(Courtesy, Lisa Williams, Pennsylvania Game Commission)**

ing a 3/4-inch-wide horizontal ventilation slot in the rear of each, another roosting chamber is added, with access from either house or the sides. An exceptional temperature range is provided for bats to choose from, with reduced danger of overheating. In climates where high temperatures in July average 100°F or more, extra protection can be provided by extending the overhang of the metal roof to lengthen the period of midday shade.

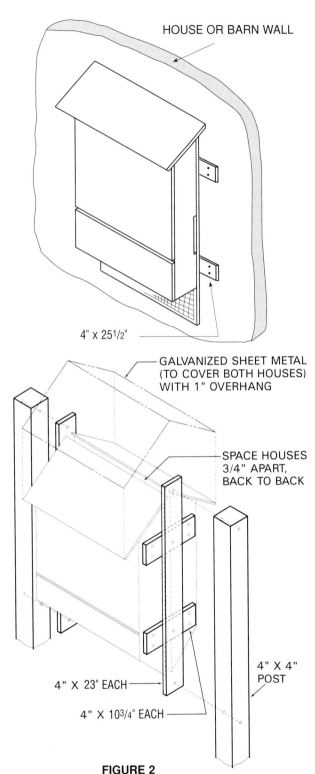

HOUSE OR BARN WALL

4" x 25½"

GALVANIZED SHEET METAL
(TO COVER BOTH HOUSES)
WITH 1" OVERHANG

SPACE HOUSES
3/4" APART,
BACK TO BACK

4" X 4"
POST

4" X 23" EACH

4" X 10¾" EACH

FIGURE 2

Nursery houses can be mounted independently on the side of a building or on a pole. However, when houses are mounted back to back in pairs, the space between can accommodate more bats and provides an especially well-ventilated area for use on hot days. The tin roof is optional, but aids greatly in protecting the houses from midday sun.

Habitat

Most nursery colonies of bats choose roosts within ¼ mile of water, preferably a stream, river, or lake. Greatest bat house success has been achieved in areas of diverse habitat, especially where there is a mixture of differing agricultural use and natural vegetation.

Little brown and other myotis bats are most likely to use bat houses that are located nearest caves or abandoned mines that provide suitable overwintering habitat. In contrast, big brown bats can hibernate in buildings, cliff-face crevices, and other non-cave locations; free-tailed and twilight bats migrate south for winter. Bat houses are also more likely to succeed in areas where bats are most frequently found in buildings, particularly where bats have been excluded from buildings.

Mounting

Bats find houses mounted on poles or buildings more than twice as fast as those on trees. Trees may be less preferable, in part, because tree-mounted houses tend to receive less sun and may be more vulnerable to predators. Houses mounted under the eaves on wood or stone buildings, but still exposed to the sun, tend to be better protected from rain and predators and have been especially successful.

Nursery colonies of up to 400 bats have been attracted to pairs of nursery houses mounted back-to-back, ¾-inch apart on poles, both covered by a tin roof (see Figure 2). Generally, bat houses should be mounted 15-20 feet above ground, though 10-12 feet may suffice. The best locations are along the borders of streams, rivers, or lakes or along a forest edge, because these are natural bat flyways.

Protection from predators

Safety from predators appears to be a key factor in bat choice, and houses mounted on sides of buildings or high up on poles provide the best protection. The largest colonies attract the most predators and therefore require the greatest height. Locations at least 20-25 feet from trees reduce obstructions and predation and may receive more necessary sunlight.

In areas where climbing snakes occur, it may be necessary to purchase predator guards from a supplier of purple martin house products. You may make your own guards by tightly covering the upper end of a 2-foot section of 10-inch-diameter galvanized stove pipe with ½-inch hardware cloth, allowing a hole in the middle for a bat house pole. Place one such predator guard around each pole about four feet above the ground. You may further thwart climbing invaders by occasionally oiling the exterior metal. Snakes typically attempt to climb the inner pole to the screen and give up. If mounting on tree trunks, remember that trees out in the open with large diameters and relatively smooth bark are the safest from snakes and other climbing predators. If bats suddenly disappear at a time when they traditionally have been present, the most likely culprits are rat snakes, though other predators can have the same effect.

Avoiding uninvited guests
Houses with open bottoms are far less likely to be occupied by birds, mice, squirrels, or parasites, and they do not require removal of accumulated droppings. Wasps do not normally cause problems once bat colonies move into bat houses. Paper wasps, the ones with painful stings, do not build nests in $3/4$-inch spaces. If they begin to build a nest at a house entrance, they can be discouraged with blasts of water from a high pressure hose before their workers emerge. Mud daubers are seldom aggressive and have weak stings. If their nests accumulate prior to bat occupancy, just scrape or hose them out in the fall or winter.

Importance of local experimentation
We have much to learn about the needs of individual bat species in differing climates. It is important to test for local needs before putting up more than a few houses, especially comparing different sun exposures and shades of a color for heat absorption.

To determine the temperature needs of local bats, check to see what colors and sun exposures are recommended. Then try mounting two houses side by side on a building where they receive similar sun, but paint one darker than the other to see which one the bats prefer. Alternatively, paint one pair of pole-mounted houses darker than another pair, or extend the roof to provide more shade. Finally, when bats move in, observe their behavior to see which house or pair of houses they prefer during temperature extremes through a daily or seasonal cycle. Their choices will provide important clues to their needs, enabling you to enjoy improved success with future houses.

Ideas for the future

NUMEROUS IDEAS REMAIN to be tried. If you're an inventor, don't let our design suggestions interfere with your imagination. Do remember that temperature, a secure gripping surface, and safety from predators are all important for bats, as well as proximity to ample food and water.

So far, we have attempted to accommodate only crevice-roosting species with the three designs shown in this handbook. Other bats may prefer different designs altogether, such as long narrow tubes or much larger roost chamber dimensions. Endangered Indiana bats, and many other species, roost under exfoliating tree bark in the summer. Success in attracting such bats may be as simple as encircling a tree trunk with a 24- to 36-inch piece of sheet metal, plastic, fiberglass, or tar paper. Attach it as tightly as possible at the top, allowing it to flare out an inch or two at the bottom. Corrugated sheet metal, wrapped around trees to protect wood duck nesting boxes from predators, has proved highly successful in attracting nursery colonies of little brown bats. Bats apparently move around the trunk to find the needed amount of solar heating.

In lowland desert areas, where bats have difficulty finding roosts that are cool enough, you might try making bat houses out of lightweight mixtures of concrete. Such houses, thus far used only in Europe, may be especially well adapted to meet the needs of bats that roost in desert rock crevices. Concrete houses can be formed to provide a central crevice with an open bottom. Successful houses have even been constructed from $1/4$-inch plastic conduit material. One nursery house design, made entirely of plastic, with $1/4$-inch plastic mesh roosting partitions, recently attracted 700 Mexican free-tailed bats in Texas. Provision of $3/4$-inch vent holes, covered with plastic shields to block light, were essential to success. Recent evidence shows that even styrofoam houses can be successful. However, when using any white material in construction, the interior should be painted black to ensure the darkness that bats prefer.

Most European bat houses are built with bottoms; however, these require regular cleaning and harbor more parasites than those with open bottoms. An average painted bat house may last for 10 years or more, considerably longer than most people today remain in one place. By using open-bottom designs, even bat houses abandoned by their builders will remain available to bats for a long time.

Although much remains to be learned, it is encouraging that even the less sophisticated bat houses, mounted singly and without screening on the partitions, already are averaging more than 80 percent occupancy when ideally located relative to solar exposure and habitat. We strongly encourage you to experiment and become an active participant in BCI's North American Bat House Research Project.

SMALL ECONOMY BAT HOUSE

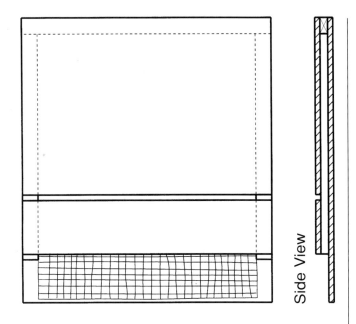

Side View

Materials Needed (makes 1)

1/4 sheet (2' x 4') 1/2" cdx (outdoor grade) plywood
1 piece 1" x 2" (0.75" x 1.75" finished) x 8' pine (furring strip)
1/8" mesh HDPE (plastic) netting, 20" x 22.5"
    [such as Internet product #XV-1670 (1-800-328-8456)]
20-30 1 5/8" multipurpose (drywall) screws
1 pint latex acrylic paint
1 tube paintable acrylic caulk
5/16" staples

Recommended tools

table saw or handsaw	caulking gun
variable speed reversing drill	scissors
Phillips bit for drill	stapler
tape measure or yardstick	paintbrush

Construction procedure

1. Measure and cut plywood into three pieces:
   26.5" x 24"   16.5" x 24"   5" x 24"
2. Measure and cut furring into one 24" and two 20 1/4" pieces.
3. Screw back to furring, caulking first. Start with 24" piece at top.
4. Staple the netting to inside surface of back, starting at the bottom. Be sure netting lies flat (curve down) and does not pucker.
5. Screw front to furring, top piece first (don't forget to caulk). Leave 1/2" vent space between top and bottom front pieces.
6. Caulk around outside joints if needed to seal roosting chamber.
7. Attach a 3" x 28" board to the top as a roof, if desired.
8. Paint exterior at least twice.

Optional Modifications to the Small Economy Bat House

1. Wider bat houses can be built for larger colonies. Be sure to adjust dimensions for back and front pieces, ceiling furring strip, and netting. A 3/4" support spacer may be required in the center of the roosting chamber for bat houses over 24" wide.
2. Two bat houses can be placed back-to-back mounted on poles. Before assembly, a horizontal 3/4" slot should be cut in the back of each house about 10" from the bottom edge of the back piece to improve ventilation and permit movement of bats between houses. Two pieces of wood, 4" x 4 1/4" x 3/4", screwed horizontally to each side will join the two boxes. One 3" x 22" vertical piece, attached to each side over the horizontal pieces, blocks light but allows bats and air to enter. Leave a 3/4" space between the two houses, and roughen the wood surfaces or cover the back of each with plastic netting. Do not cover the vents. A tin roof covering both houses protects them and helps prevent overheating. Eaves should be about 3" in southern areas and about 1 1/2" in the North.
3. Ventilation may not be necessary in colder climates. In this case, the front should be a single piece 23" long. Smaller bat houses should not be used in northern areas.

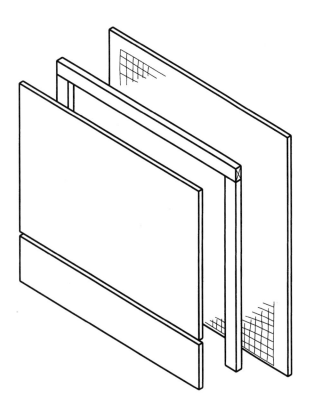

FIGURE 3

LARGE ECONOMY BAT HOUSE

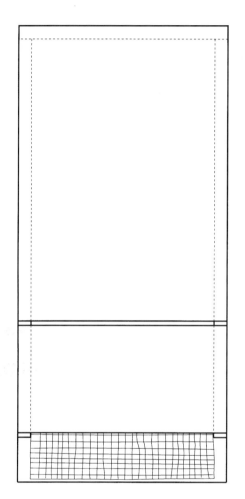

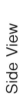

Side View

Materials Needed (makes 1)

1/2 sheet (2' x 8') 1/2" cdx (outdoor grade) plywood
2 pieces 1" x 2" (0.75" x 1.75" finished) x 8' pine (furring strips)
1/8" mesh HDPE (plastic) netting, 20" x 49"
    [such as Internet product #XV-1670 (1-800-328-8456)]
40-50 1 5/8" multipurpose (drywall) screws
1 quart latex acrylic paint
1 tube paintable acrylic caulk
5/16" staples

Recommended tools

table saw or handsaw	caulking gun
variable speed reversing drill	scissors
Phillips bit for drill	stapler
tape measure or yardstick	paintbrush

Construction procedure

1. Measure and cut plywood into three pieces:
    51" x 24"   33" x 24"   12" x 24"
2. Measure and cut furring into one 24" and two 43 3/4" pieces.
3. Screw back to furring, caulking first. Start with 24" piece at top.
4. Staple the netting to inside surface of back, starting at the bottom. Be sure netting lies flat (curve down) and does not pucker.
5. Screw front to furring, top piece first (don't forget to caulk). Leave 1/2" vent space between top and bottom front pieces.
6. Caulk around outside joints if needed to seal roosting chamber.
7. Attach a 4" x 28" board to the top as a roof, if desired.
8. Paint exterior at least twice.

Optional Modifications to the Large Economy Bat House

1. Wider bat houses can be built for larger colonies. Be sure to adjust dimensions for back and front pieces, ceiling furring strip, and netting. A 3/4" support spacer may be required in the center of the roosting chamber for bat houses over 24" wide.

2. Two bat houses can be placed back-to-back mounted on poles. Before assembly, a horizontal 3/4" slot should be cut in the back of each house about 17" from the bottom edge of the back piece to improve ventilation and permit movement of bats between houses. Two pieces of wood, 4" x 4 1/4" x 3/4", screwed horizontally to each side will join the two boxes. One 3" x 45" vertical piece, attached to each side over the horizontal pieces, blocks light but allows bats and air to enter. Leave a 3/4" space between the two houses, and roughen the wood surfaces or cover the back of each with plastic netting. Do not cover the vents. A tin roof covering both houses protects them and helps prevent overheating. Eaves should be about 3" in southern areas and about 1 1/2" in the North.

3. Ventilation may not be necessary in colder climates. In this case, the front should be a single piece 45" long.

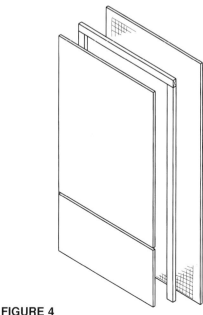

FIGURE 4

NURSERY HOUSE

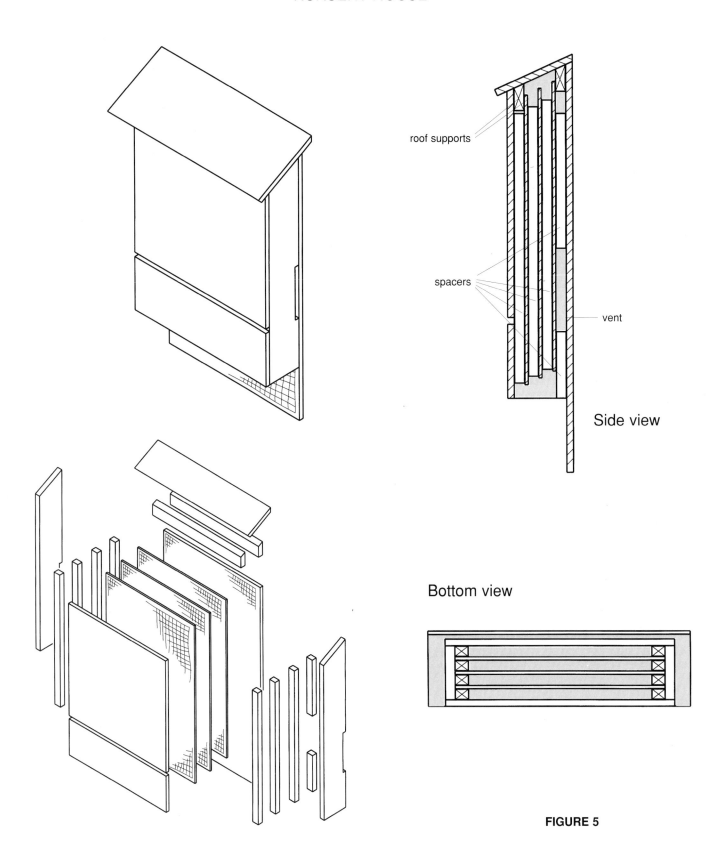

roof supports

spacers

vent

Side view

Bottom view

FIGURE 5

NURSERY HOUSE

Materials Needed (makes 2)

See cutting diagrams on pages 14-15.

1/2 sheet (4' x 4') 1/2" cdx (outdoor grade) plywood

1/2 sheet (4' x 4') 1/4" cdx (outdoor grade) plywood

2 pieces 1" x 6" (0.75" x 5.25" finished) x 8' pine or cedar

1/8" mesh HDPE (plastic) netting, 7' x 36"
[such as Internet product #XV-1670 (1-800-328-8456)]

1 lb. 1 5/8" multipurpose (drywall) screws

1 quart latex acrylic paint

1 tube paintable acrylic caulk

5/16" staples

Recommended tools

table saw	scissors
variable speed reversing drill	stapler
Phillips bit for drill	paintbrush
tape measure or yardstick	bar clamp (optional)
caulking gun	sander (optional)

Construction procedure

1. Measure and mark all wood as per cutting diagrams on pages 14-15. Cut out all parts.

2. Cut six pieces of netting 14" x 21". Staple to partitions.

3. Screw back to sides, caulking first. Be sure top angles match.

4. Cut a piece of netting 16" x 30" and staple to inside surface of back, starting at the bottom. Be sure netting lies flat (curve down) and does not pucker.

5. Attach 5" and 10" spacers to inside corners as per drawings on page 12.

6. Place a partition on spacers to within 1/2" of roof. Place 20" spacers on partition, screw to first spacers (through partition). Be careful not to block side vents.

7. Repeat step 6 for remaining partitions and spacers.

8. Screw front to sides, top piece first (don't forget to caulk). Be sure top angles match (sand if necessary). Leave 1/2" vent space between top and bottom front pieces. A bar clamp may be useful if sides have flared out during construction.

9. Attach roof supports to the top inside of front and back pieces. Be careful that screws do not protrude into roosting chamber.

10. Caulk around all top surfaces, sanding first if necessary to ensure good fit with roof.

11. Screw roof to sides and roof supports. Caulk around outside of roof if needed to seal roosting chamber.

12. Paint exterior at least twice.

Optional Modifications to the Nursery House

1. Wider bat houses can be built for larger colonies. Be sure to adjust dimensions for back and front pieces, roof, partitions, roof supports, and netting. Additional spacers may be required in the center of the roosting chamber for bat houses over 24" wide. You will no longer be able to get two bat houses from two half sheets of plywood.

2. Taller bat houses can also be created by adjusting the dimensions of the front and back pieces, partitions, sides, spacers, and netting. Bat houses 3' or taller should have the horizontal vent slot 12" from the bottom of the roosting chamber.

3. Longer landing platforms (up to 12") can be substituted, but they should still be covered with plastic screening.

4. Two bat houses can be placed back-to-back mounted on poles. Before assembly, a horizontal 3/4" slot should be cut in the back of each house about 12" from the bottom edge of the back piece to improve ventilation and permit movement of bats between houses. Two pieces of wood, 4" x 10 3/4" x 3/4", screwed horizontally to each side will join the two boxes. One 4" x 23" vertical piece, attached to each side over the horizontal pieces, blocks light but allows bats and air to enter. Leave a 3/4" space between the two houses, and roughen the wood surfaces, or cover the back of each with plastic netting. Do not cover the vents. A tin roof covering both houses protects them and helps prevent overheating. Eaves should be about 3" in southern areas and about 1 1/2" in the North. See figure 2 on page 8 for illustrations.

5. Ventilation may not be necessary in colder climates. In this case, the front of this bat house should be a single piece 23" long. Far northern bat houses may also benefit from a partial bottom to help retain heat. Leave a 3/4" entry gap at the back, and be sure the bottom does not interfere with access to the front crevices. A hinged bottom and regular maintenance is required to prevent guano buildup.

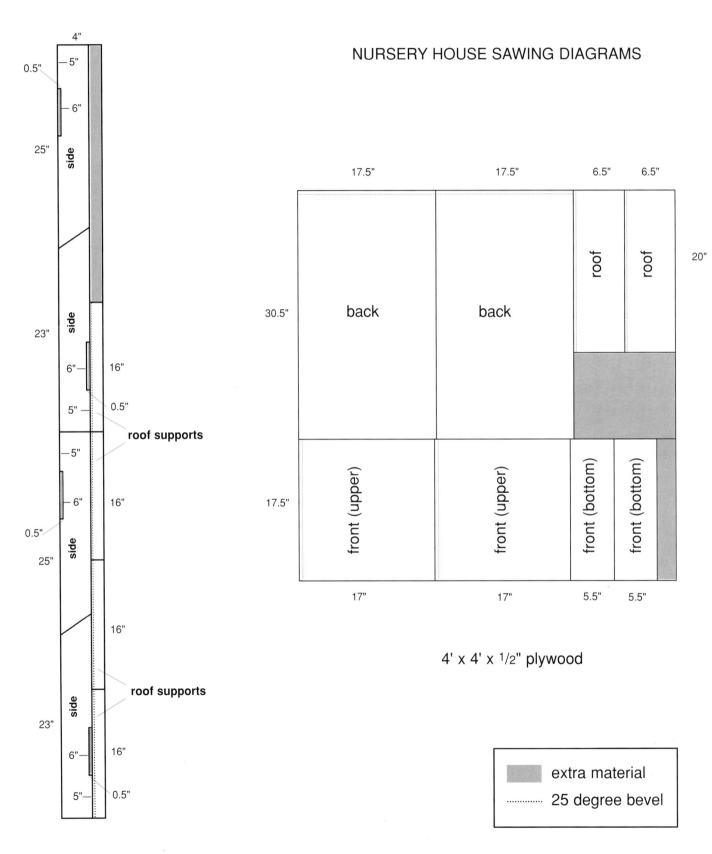

NURSERY HOUSE SAWING DIAGRAMS

4" · 0.5" · 5" · 6" · 25" · side · 23" · side · 6" · 16" · 5" · 0.5" · **roof supports** · 5" · 6" · 16" · 0.5" · side · 25" · 16" · **roof supports** · side · 23" · 6" · 16" · 5" · 0.5"

1" x 6" x 8' sheeting

17.5" · 17.5" · 6.5" · 6.5"
30.5" · back · back · roof · roof · 20"
17.5" · front (upper) · front (upper) · front (bottom) · front (bottom)
17" · 17" · 5.5" · 5.5"

4' x 4' x 1/2" plywood

▨ extra material
⋯⋯ 25 degree bevel

FIGURE 6

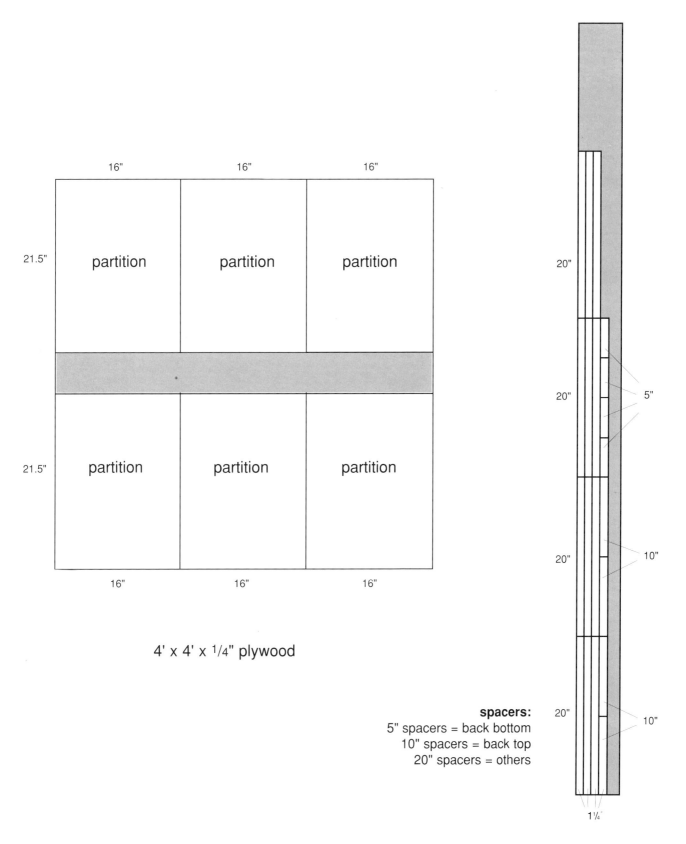

16"   16"   16"

21.5"   partition   partition   partition

21.5"   partition   partition   partition

16"   16"   16"

4' x 4' x ¼" plywood

20"

20"   5"

20"   10"

spacers:
5" spacers = back bottom
10" spacers = back top
20" spacers = others

20"   10"

1¼"

1" x 6" x 8' sheeting

A Few Pointers for Bat House Experimenters

Attention to seemingly small details can make a big difference to bat house success . . .

• *Bat house success* is dramatically enhanced when houses are: 1) caulked and painted to be airtight and watertight; 2) colored and hung to best meet local needs for solar heating; 3) mounted 15-20 feet or higher on buildings or poles at least 20-25 feet from the nearest trees; 4) located near rivers, lakes, or ponds, especially along water or forest edges or in areas where varied agriculture is mixed with natural habitat. Small commercial houses are often poorly designed for bats and sold without instruction, greatly reducing overall success. However, people who build their own houses and carefully locate them according to the instructions provided here are achieving high levels of success (see "The Secrets of Bat House Success," page 17).

• *Local testing* is required before putting up large numbers of bat houses in any new area. Temperature is a critical consideration. First tests can be accomplished by: 1) mounting houses in pairs on buildings, one darker, the other lighter; 2) varying the amount or timing of exposure to heating from the sun; 3) comparing pole-mounted back-to-back pairs in darker versus lighter shades of a color or with longer and shorter roof overhangs to vary solar heating; 4) orienting pairs on poles to increase temperature ranges by facing them north/south or to facilitate greater stability by facing them east/west; 5) mounting three to four houses around the trunk of an exceptionally large tree, out in the open (at least 10 feet from nearest branches) to receive varied sun.

• *First occupancy,* in the majority of successful bat houses, occurs in the first new summer season after placement, meaning that houses put up in fall or winter are most likely to be used during the next summer. About half attract bats within two summers. Nursery colonies often begin with just one or a few individuals the first season, greatly expanding over the next two seasons.

• *Cleaning* of open-bottomed houses is unnecessary unless mud dauber nests accumulate.

• *Maintenance* should not be needed for the first several years for houses that have been carefully caulked and painted before being put up. However, eventual recaulking and painting may be necessary and should be done during the off-season when bats are not present. Drafty houses may be abandoned if not repaired. Houses mounted on fast growing trees may require periodic rehanging; they should be checked at least every second year.

• *Annual use cycles* may range from just a few weeks to entire summers in cool climates. In warmer southern areas, such as Florida and Texas, bats may use houses from February to November or even year-round. In all but the warmest climates, bats probably will begin arriving in April or May, sometimes not until early June, and may depart anytime from July to October. Use patterns are typically repeated from year to year. Sometimes annual use periods can be greatly extended by providing better temperature ranges, warmer or cooler houses, or several houses close together.

• *Observing roosting bats* is quite simple if you shine a bright light up into the open bottom. For houses mounted high up, you may need to have someone shine a light while you look with binoculars. Make observations as brief as possible at first to avoid disturbance. Once a colony is established, bats typically are quite tolerant of people looking at them as long as you do not touch the mounting poles or houses and do not shine bright lights for more than 10 seconds.

• *Counting bats* may be relatively easy by simply looking inside if there are just a few, but when larger colonies become established the only reasonably accurate method is to count them emerging at dusk. To determine if you have a nursery colony, briefly look inside after the adults emerge. Young are always left behind over a roughly 3-week period until they learn to fly, normally in June in moderate climates, May in the warmest, and July in the coolest.

• *Testing bat needs* is relatively easy once even a few move into one of your houses. Provide them nearby houses with more or less sun, darker or lighter color, improved landing areas, rougher climbing surfaces, paired houses with greater temperature ranges, etc. Careful observations of daily and seasonal movements within and between houses during cool versus hot periods can provide vital knowledge about how best to help your local bats, and by sharing such information, you can contribute greatly to progress.

The Secrets of Bat House Success

SINCE BAT CONSERVATION INTERNATIONAL first popularized bat houses in the early 1980s, thousands have been erected in backyards, parks, and forests all across America. Yet nothing in the history of bat conservation efforts has generated more controversy. Claims and counterclaims over whether bat houses work too often have been based only on limited local observations. As a result, many erroneous conclusions have been reached about the overall success or failure of bat houses. We now know a great deal more, thanks to the many BCI members and friends who are testing and reporting bat house use under a wide variety of conditions and geographical locations.

To evaluate the rate of bat house occupancy and why bats prefer some houses over others, in 1992 BCI conducted a comprehensive survey of 420 people in 26 states in the United States and one province in Canada who had built or purchased one or more bat houses. Some of the results were surprising, opening the door for further experimentation. But the most encouraging news is how successful bat houses really are: 52 percent of the houses in our survey attracted bats (study details begin on page 24). The survey also enabled us to quantify roosting preferences over broad geographical areas for the first time.

It is clear from this study that when bat houses are placed to meet bat needs, occupancy success is high. Taking the survey results for the northern third of the United States, where we found bat houses are most used and are now best understood, we checked to see what the success rate was for houses that met just two of the most important criteria. We looked at all houses located a quarter of a mile or less from a stream or river, or a lake larger than three acres, and receiving at least four or more hours of sun daily. The occupancy rate for these houses, without consideration of other factors, was 83 percent. When we further limited the sample by adding houses stained or painted dark, occupancy rose to 92 percent (this proved important for heat gain in northern latitudes). When we added another condition—houses located in areas of mixed agriculture (mostly orchards)—100 percent of the 13 houses meeting all four criteria were occupied. For reasons as yet unknown, bats seemed to be especially attracted to such areas.

Two bat house builders from different parts of the country illustrate the high occupancy rates that can be expected when bat needs are met. Both locations are

In bat houses where the species could be positively identified, little brown bats were the most common.

A BCI study on bat house use in the United States reveals that bats are occupying bat houses season after season in record numbers . . .

ROBIN MICHAL KOONTZ

Tony Koch put up nine special bat houses in the loft of his barn to create a more hospitable environment for nursing mother bats. These unusual houses have open sides because of the warmth of the loft. Mother bats routinely move their pups from house to house, perhaps to escape parasites.

near rivers and are surrounded by a mixture of orchards, other agriculture, and woodlands. Tony Koch, an organic farmer in Oregon, has had 23 of 24 bat houses occupied by a growing colony of more than 2,000 little brown bats. Koch's houses are stained or painted dark brown or black and are exposed to six or more hours of daily sun. His only failure was a shaded house on a tree, illustrating the importance of solar heating in the North. In the South, Baxter and Carol Adams of Texas have attracted approximately 1,000 Mexican free-tailed bats, which occupy all five of their bat houses.

Innovations and new discoveries

MOST BAT HOUSES SURVEYED were either purchased from BCI or patterned after BCI designs, but several innovative people developed modifications that will substantially improve our ability to attract larger colonies. The fact that bat houses only 24 inches tall and wide, and 5 or 6 inches deep, can attract nursery colonies of as many as 200 to 300 bats is very good news. Since such houses require far less time and expense to build, and on the average attract more bats than the much larger Missouri-style houses,* it is no longer necessary to build these costly houses to provide for large colonies.

The Adamses of Texas experimented with screening, a material bats find especially easy to cling to, and this may explain why two of their houses, with interior dimensions of only about 16 inches by 7 1/2 inches by 5 1/2 inches and two vertical partitions, each shelter up to 150 Mexican free-tailed bats. They lined the vertical partitions with fiberglass insect (or window) screening, which is still intact after five years. (Because fiberglass window screening is highly variable in quality, and often wears out rapidly or sags to obstruct roosting spaces, we now recommend 1/8-inch or 1/4-inch heavy-duty plastic screening of the kind sold by Internet, Inc., 1-800-328-8456.)

Quarter-inch hardware cloth has been used successfully by Dr. Stephen Frantz, a research scientist for the New York Department of Health. He noticed that nursery colonies in attics showed a distinct preference for roosting on hardware cloth. Frantz believes that, in some bat houses, it could be used instead of wood partitions to increase roosting space and permit a colony to remain in closer contact. He attracted over 300 little brown bats to a house of this design that he construct-

* A very large free-standing bat house developed by the Missouri Department of Conservation in the early 1980s. Because of its size and cost, it has been built mostly by parks and nature centers.

MERLIN D. TUTTLE

Pallid bats were among those found in bat houses in the Southwest. Although bat houses in lowland desert regions may become too hot for most bats, those placed against shaded buildings, especially stone, have had some success.

ed. Frantz also built another successful house by covering wooden partitions with tar paper held in place by hardware cloth. The tar paper was added to help absorb and retain heat. Heavy-duty plastic screening of the type sold by Internet, Inc., will last longer, is nontoxic, and has been successfully used in place of wooden partitions.

All available evidence suggests that most of America's crevice-roosting bats prefer crevice widths of 3/4-inch to 1 inch when using open-bottomed houses. However, they also routinely use bat houses with a single 2-inch chamber and a 3/4-inch entry. Koch reported that wasps were less attracted to 3/4-inch roosting crevices, which he now uses exclusively. Lisa Williams, of State College, Pennsylvania, conducted research on bat houses in collaboration with Cal Butchkoski of the Pennsylvania Game Commission. They added ventila-

MERLIN D. TUTTLE

Big brown bats were found hibernating in bat houses as far north as New York. Such use may be increased with the addition of insulation in bat houses.

tion slots that provided wider temperature ranges, thereby increasing use.

In an attempt to attract bats faster, some people painted new bat houses with a mixture of bat guano and water, but there is no clear documentation that this increased success. Koch used guano from the same species and vicinity and consistently attracted bats the first season, while houses made of new, untreated wood were twice ignored until the second season. But other builders, who did not treat with guano, also attracted bats the first season, some immediately. To treat their houses, people sometimes buy bat guano or obtain it from caves. This, however, could prove counterproductive because droppings from one species may not attract, and might even repel, another species. Since bats in this study were shown to prefer aged wood, it is possible that merely filling the inside of a house with slightly damp earth or a rich humus and then pouring it out after a few days would work just as well.

The study also revealed that the higher a bat house is located, the greater the occupancy success. Mounting houses on poles can help accommodate bat preferences for roosts 15 to 20 feet or higher and offers ideal opportunities to take advantage of solar heating, especially in northern areas. A further advantage of poles is pro-

tection from predators. Predation at bat houses was not included in the scope of this study, but instinctual fear of predators may explain bat preferences for higher roosting sites. Dr. Frantz notes that, where raccoons are a problem, poles can be wrapped with an 18-inch piece of sheet metal three feet above the ground. Even in the wild, bats often have difficulty finding safe roosts. We recently checked thousands of desert rock crevices for roosting bats and found that despite an abundance of cliff-face crevices, bats often found very few they could use. Their consistent preference was for places unreachable by snakes or small mammal predators.

The advantages of multiple bat houses

THE MOST SUCCESSFUL bat house builders we surveyed erected their houses in groups of three or more. Some observed nursery colonies move their young among the different houses. This was especially well documented by Williams and Butchkoski. They placed bat houses in groups of three, just a few feet apart on the sides of buildings, and carefully monitored internal temperatures. The bats moved their young into the coolest houses on hot days and into the warmest houses on cool days. In addition, mothers sometimes moved young back and forth even when temperature seemed not to be a factor, a phenomenon also observed by Tony Koch in his nine nursery roosts. Occasional moves may additionally help bats evade parasites.

Robert Ginn places his Georgia bat houses in groups

of three on trees, one facing south and one each facing northwest and northeast. Twenty-six of his 29 houses are occupied. The three that remain empty are mounted just one to a tree. Close placement of two or three houses painted different colors or positioned to absorb varying amounts of solar heat appears to help attract nursery colonies and also provides excellent opportunities for studying bat temperature needs. Such groupings may prove ideal in areas where temperature requirements are poorly understood.

In the hottest climates bats typically roost in rock or concrete crevices, which act as heat sinks to help keep them from overheating. Bat biologist Dr. Patricia Brown reports that lowland desert bats seldom roost in buildings, meaning that they also may not occupy bat houses in areas of intense heat. Careful experimentation with insulation, reflective paints, and heat sinks will be essential to success in these areas. Both pallid and free-tailed bats have used bat houses mounted on the shaded sides of stone buildings in extra-hot climates. However, at least in central Texas, free-tails and cave myotis appear to prefer houses exposed to at least six hours of daily sun.

The considerable success that some people in our survey had with bat houses was not without patient observation and experimentation before they put up large numbers of them. Much of the controversy over whether bat houses work is stimulated by well-intentioned but premature large-scale projects. Many of these have a high probability of failure largely because of poor placement and lack of prior testing to evaluate bat roosting needs in a particular area.

Many people experiment with bat houses out of a desire to find a natural means of reducing local populations of mosquitoes and other insect pests. Nevertheless, simply erecting large numbers of bat houses to solve a town's mosquito problems is unlikely to succeed. No mosquito control is 100 percent effective, and a pesticide-free approach most often requires a broad range of treatment, including elimination of artificial breeding sites, and use of a variety of natural predators, from small fish and aquatic insects to bats.

Bat biologist Dr. Elizabeth Pierson voiced concern that large-scale bat house projects might be considered by forestry personnel as adequate mitigation for proposed destruction of natural habitats. While there is certainly great potential in developing artificial roosts for more bats, we currently know little about the needs of most American species and cannot yet assume that existing houses meet the needs of more than a relative few.

Owners of multiple bat houses reported that their bats often switched roosts when temperatures became extreme. In Lisa Williams' well-documented study, bats moved their young into the coolest houses on hot days and into the warmest houses on cool days among these three different designs.

In some circumstances, you may be able to provide unique roosting habitat for bats. These guards were put up to protect nesting wood ducks from predators and have housed nursery colonies of little brown bats for more than 25 years.

R. L. CLAWSON

By putting up bat houses and carefully observing the results, we have an excellent opportunity to help bats and to learn more about their needs.

The value of bat houses to conservation

SINCE BCI FIRST MARKETED bat houses in 1986, many other vendors have followed suit.** While some have done much to increase public interest in bat conservation, others pay far more attention to competitive pricing than to bat needs. Such vendors rarely provide mounting instructions or other accurate information and often market poorly constructed houses, which are unlikely to be used even under the best of circumstances. As a result, genuine bat conservation efforts suffer.

By putting up bat houses and carefully observing the results, we have an excellent opportunity to help bats and to learn more about their needs. If your bat house is unoccupied, experiment! Based on what we now know, unoccupied houses often become successful

** The only commercial bat houses on the U.S. market today that directly benefit BCI's bat conservation efforts are sold through Plow and Hearth of Orange, Virginia, and the BCI catalogue. These houses are continually improved to incorporate new discoveries.

if they are moved only a few feet to receive more or less sun, are stained or painted to absorb or reflect heat, or are merely raised. Occupancy of previously unsuccessful houses, after modification, provides especially enlightening insights into bat needs.

If, despite providing ideal conditions, a bat house remains unoccupied, there could be other reasons why. Most properly built and placed houses in our survey were occupied. However some likely fail because local bats already have all the roosts they need. Distances to undisturbed hibernating sites, local pollution levels, and food base are also important factors. With the possible exception of lowland desert areas, we know of no evidence suggesting that any geographic region is unsuitable for successful bat house use.

The value of building artificial roosts is already well documented for birds. The U.S. population of purple martins grew by more than 25 percent from 1966 to 1986, while almost all other insectivorous songbirds suffered significant declines. Bluebirds, for which a major nest box program was also established, were also

an exception. The largest songbird losses were among cavity nesters, especially those that, like bats, do not make their own nest holes.

Some of our most endangered bats, such as the tree-roosting Indiana bat, may be helped by simple use of metal, tar paper, or even fiberglass or plastic collars around tree trunks. In addition, we now know that the big brown bat, one of North America's most agriculturally valuable species, can live year-round in some bat houses. With experimentation, such as using insulation, we may be able to increase the odds of providing year-round roosts for this and other species.

Bat Conservation International's North American Bat House Research Project will provide invaluable observations and stimulate the experiments required to

Some species that would not ordinarily roost in a bat house, such as this endangered Indiana bat, may be helped by the use of metal or other collars wrapped around tree trunks. Corrugated metal imitates the exfoliating bark that these bats prefer for their summer roosts, but metal is far more durable. Other materials, from plastic or fiberglass to tar paper, may also be used.

better understand bat roosting preferences. As bats increasingly lose their traditional roosts, such studies become all the more critical.

How Research Findings Reveal Bat Preferences

New knowledge of bat preferences opens many opportunities to improve bat house occupancy success . . .

CAREFUL READING OF the detailed findings of BCI's bat house survey before you begin your own bat house project will greatly increase your chances of success.

Occupancy rates—BCI members achieved significantly higher success rates (64 percent) than the generally less informed nonmembers (44 percent). Nonmembers had often built or purchased bat houses without adequate instructions, and they were 10 percent more likely to use the smallest, least successful sizes. The average occupancy rate was 52 percent. However, as bat house users become better informed, higher success can be expected.

Use rates varied among the six basic bat house models (Figure 7), larger houses tending to be chosen over smaller ones. Bats preferred the tallest houses with the longest crevices, oriented side to side, within the size range investigated.

Eleven bat houses that relied on basically the same designs as Models 3, 5, and 6, but that provided longer roosting chambers, had the highest occupancy rate at 73 percent. These houses averaged 24 inches to 36 inches tall x 16 inches to 24 inches wide x 4 inches to 5 inches deep or 12 inches tall x 32 inches wide x 5 1/2 inches deep.

Missouri-style bat houses, approximately 7 feet 6 inches long, 4 feet wide, and 2 feet 6 inches tall, with entry through an open bottom, were only 39 percent occupied when built according to instructions. The use rate was surprisingly low for such a large house. This design apparently fails to meet several key needs. In northern areas, the sun probably does not sufficiently warm the roosting crevices, because the design calls for a spacious attic that shades the chambers from the sun's warmth. Equally important, each of its 3/4-inch wide roosting chambers is only 12 inches tall and long, meaning that bat colonies are forced to divide into many small groups, unable to share body heat. This gives them little or no advantage over the smallest houses illustrated. Furthermore, in southern areas where some shading from solar heating might be advantageous, Missouri-style houses are generally too heavy and cumbersome to be placed high enough on poles to attract free-tailed bats, one of the most common species in the South.

Colony sizes—Ninety-four percent of colony size estimates were based on visual inspection through open bat house bottoms. Comparison of counts made of

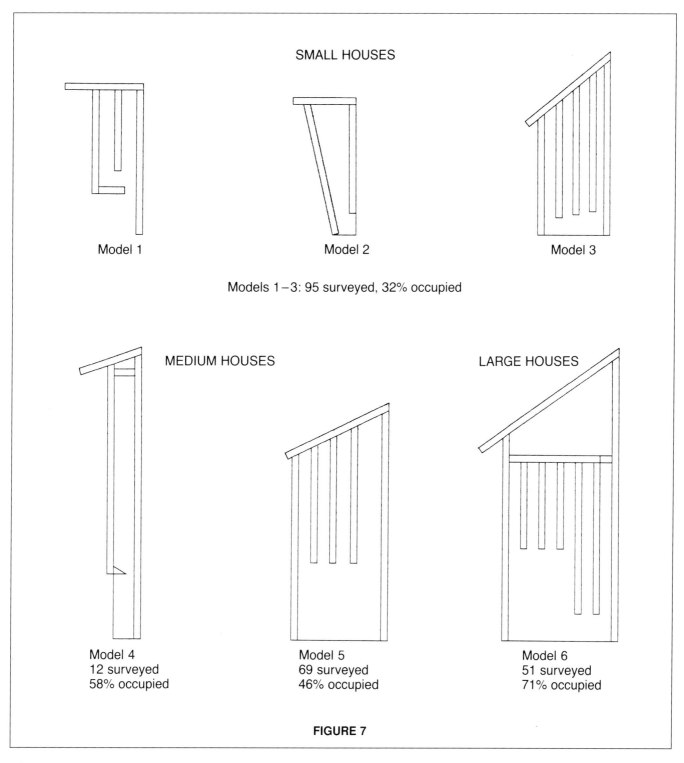

SMALL HOUSES

Model 1   Model 2   Model 3

Models 1–3: 95 surveyed, 32% occupied

MEDIUM HOUSES   LARGE HOUSES

Model 4
12 surveyed
58% occupied

Model 5
69 surveyed
46% occupied

Model 6
51 surveyed
71% occupied

FIGURE 7

The majority of bat houses in the survey were patterned after these six basic designs, which have appeared in various BCI pub-
lications over the past 10 years. To determine the effect of size on occupancy success, they were further grouped into four basic
size categories, each of which had many variations. As shown, certain designs were more successful in attracting bats than
others, but larger size, especially providing longer and taller roosting chambers, appeared to be an important factor.

roosting, versus emerging, bats showed that the former and predominantly used method underestimated real numbers by approximately 38 percent—because bats cluster toward the top where observers often cannot see the innermost individuals.

Colony sizes for small bat house Models 1 to 3 averaged 28 bats and ranged from one to 150, though the most frequently reported numbers were just one to five. Colony sizes for the medium-sized Model 4 houses averaged 21 bats and were used most frequently by colonies of 21 to 30 bats; the largest colony sizes reported for this model were between 31 and 50 individuals. Model 5 houses averaged 14 bats per house and were used by from one to 150 bats. Colonies attracted to Model 6 houses averaged 29 bats and ranged from one to 250.

A surprising number of houses shelter nursery colonies, some of them 200 or more bats in a single house. This one is shared by both little brown bats and eastern long-eared myotis.

Eleven wider houses of the Model 3, 5, and 6 designs (see "Occupancy Rates" section) held average colonies of 100 bats, ranging from 13 to 250. The much larger Missouri-style house, as originally designed, averaged colonies of only 65 bats, ranging from eight to 250 per house.

Use patterns—Occupancy rates for bat houses built and put up by different people varied greatly with placement, especially when erected in areas of differing bat habitat and needs. These uneven patterns clearly explain much of the controversy over whether bat houses work and emphasize the need for broad-based sampling.

Among the eight largest samples reported by individual people who had erected multiple bat houses, use rates varied from 0 to 96 percent. For example, at one Oregon location, none of 18 houses placed on trees in dense forest were occupied, while 23 of 24 at another Oregon site attracted bats when placed both outside and inside a barn and on poles at the edge of woodlots. The only one not used was mounted on a shaded tree trunk.

Time until first occupancy—Most houses used by bats in the 1992 study were occupied in the first season. The proportion of occupancy versus time from installment was as follows:

Time Lapsed	Occupancy Rate
<1 month	24%
1 to 6 months (through 1st summer)	46%
1 year (through 2nd summer)	15%
2 years	11%
3 years	2%
4 years	1%
5 years	1%

Species occupying bat houses—Most houses studied were erected by laypeople who could only guess at a bat's identity. However, bats from 37 percent of the occupied houses were positively identified by biologists or were photographed well enough to permit identification by BCI staff. Of these, 82 percent were used by little brown bats (*Myotis lucifugus*), sharing at least 7 percent with big brown bats (*Eptesicus fuscus*) and 3 percent with eastern long-eared myotis (*M. septentrionalis*). Texas houses were mostly occupied by Mexican free-tailed bats (*Tadarida brasiliensis*) or cave myotis (*Myotis velifer*), including as many as 150 in a single small house. A colony of between 30 and 50 pallid bats (*Antrozous pallidus*) occupied a small house in Arizona.

It is highly probable that additional species occupied bat houses without being positively identified. For example, many of the bats reported from Georgia, Florida, and coastal Texas may be southeastern bats (*Myotis austroriparius*). Since the 1992 study, several colonies of up to 150 evening bats (*Nycticeius humeralis*) from Florida and Texas have been identified, and Yuma myotis (*Myotis yumanensis*) have been confirmed in bat houses from Arizona to western Canada.

How bats use bat houses—Where inspection was adequate to determine the kind of use, 33 percent of houses were used by nursery colonies, 60 percent by bachelor colonies, and 7 percent for hibernation. Most houses were not checked in winter.

Only little and big brown bats and eastern long-eared myotis were confirmed to be rearing young in bat houses, though others undoubtedly were, without

MERLIN D. TUTTLE

being identified. Since the 1992 study, nursery colonies of Mexican free-tailed bats and evening bats also have been documented.

Big brown bats, the only bats likely to hibernate in bat houses over the northern two-thirds of North America, overwintered in bat houses in Texas, Kentucky, and New York.

Effect of wood type—There is no evidence that any kind of wood yet tried is objectionable to bats. Occupancy rates from the 1992 study based on the kind of wood used were as follows (types of wood used in fewer than 10 houses are excluded from this comparison):

# Houses	Wood Used	Occupancy Rate
142	Cedar	54%
77	Pine	53%
21	Cypress	29%
19	Exterior plywood	74%

The apparent preference for plywood results from its availability in large sheets, enabling construction of the longer and taller houses that bats prefer.

Mexican free-tailed bats are the most common bat house occupants in the South. They like to roost as high as possible above ground, though houses at heights of 15 to 18 feet have been quite successful.

Effect of age of wood and treating bat houses with guano—Occupied houses made of old versus new wood were compared for timing of first use. Bats were significantly more likely to move into houses during the first season if they were made of old wood. The age of wood, however, affected only the timing of first use, not the probability of use.

One bat house builder reported that his well-established and growing colony typically expands quickly into new houses made of old wood or new wood treated with a solution of bat guano diluted with water. His bats have twice waited until the second season to occupy houses made of new, untreated wood. Droppings were collected from the same species living in the immediate vicinity. This is the only strong evidence to support the idea of earlier occupancy for guano-treated houses. Other builders report that houses made of new, untreated wood have been occupied as soon as the first night.

CAL BUTCHKOSKI

After a night of feeding, little brown bats circle and re-enter a bat house. The outside of this Pennsylvania house is covered with tar paper to absorb heat. In northern climates, dark houses proved to be significantly more successful than others.

Effect of urbanization and agriculture—Only 21 houses included in our sample were put up in an urban environment. Of these, 48 percent were used, a figure surprisingly close to the overall average.

Bats exhibited a significant preference for houses located in agricultural areas. Such houses had an occupancy rate of 88 percent, compared with the average of 52 percent for all areas combined. These areas were mainly orchards interspersed with a variety of other land uses. Samples did not include any houses placed where large areas were planted in single crops.

Effect of lakes, rivers, and streams—Bat houses located within a quarter-mile of streams or rivers had an occupancy rate of 78 percent. The size of the river was

Exposure to sun is one of the most important criteria identified for determining use of bat houses.

not a significant factor. The results indicate a significant preference for houses located near streams or rivers, even when compared with large lakes. (Very large lakes, such as Lakes Michigan or Superior, were not compared.)

Where lakes were the dominant water source, bats significantly preferred houses near those of three acres or more. These houses were 62 percent occupied versus 28 percent near ponds covering less than three acres. Bats using artificial roosts in arid areas of the Southwest likely would be less influenced by the size of water sources.

Four houses located more than a mile from a lake, river, or stream were occupied, demonstrating that success is sometimes possible even when water is not near.

Effect of paint or stain—Although bat researchers have long believed that painting or staining a bat house might repel bats, no evidence was found to support this assumption. In fact, bats living in cool areas (for purposes of comparison, at latitudes north of 40 degrees) showed a significant preference for houses with exteriors either stained dark or painted black.

Sixty-seven percent of dark-colored northern houses were occupied, compared with an occupancy rate of 44 percent for those left plain. Covering houses with tar paper achieved similarly positive results. Subsequent research shows painted houses are two and a half times more successful than unpainted houses. The appropriate shade of color for heat absorption varies with climate—see "Wood treatment" section under "Designing Better Bat Houses," on page 6.

Effect of solar radiation—Exposure to sun is one of the most important criteria identified for determining use of bat houses. Bat needs are known to vary according to geographically differing ambient temperatures, but temperature cannot be accurately predicted based on mere knowledge of latitude and altitude. For purposes of this investigation, North America was divided into three zones: 1) all localities at latitudes north of 40 degrees; 2) all localities between 35 and 40 degrees; and 3) all localities south of 35 degrees.

Bat preferences are determined through controlled testing. All aspects of the test houses are identical except the attribute being tested. These differently colored houses will test local temperature preferences.

Houses, with or without dark stain or tar paper covering, were significantly more likely to be used north of 40 degrees if they were exposed to four or more hours of sun. Those receiving more than four hours of sun were 83 percent occupied, compared to 26 percent for those with less than four hours. No amount of sun appeared to be too much for northern houses, but in interpreting results, one must consider that they mostly reflect the preferences of little brown bats. Big brown bats may prefer less.

Since the 1992 study, highly successful bat houses have been reported from both shaded and full sun locations from central Texas to Florida, perhaps reflecting differing needs among species or among nursery versus bachelor colonies. One bat house, located on the shaded side of a building in central Texas, remained unoccupied for five years, but attracted hundreds of Mexican free-tailed bats soon after being moved to a location on the same building where it received more than five hours of morning sun. In central Florida, a nursery colony of 125 evening bats abandoned its shaded house when offered a pair of dark brown houses attached back-to-back on poles in full sun (see Figure 2). The colony then expanded to become a mixed nursery colony for some 400 evening bats and Mexican free-tailed bats. Further tests are in progress to determine if these bats would prefer a lighter color in the sun.

Most southern bat houses seem to be more success-

ful if exposed to sun for at least six hours per day, and early experiments with houses mounted in pairs in full sun, as illustrated in Figure 2 (page 8), are encouraging. When first using houses in a new area, it is a good idea to provide options until local preferences are established.

Effect of height above ground—Bats clearly preferred houses that were highest above ground, but this factor may not be entirely independent of exposure to sun.

# Houses	Height	Occupancy Rate
25	<10'	40%
214	11'-15'	50%
27	16'-20'	63%
10	21'-30'	70%

Effects of dense forest and distance to nearest obstacles—The 28 bat houses located in dense forest had occupancy rates significantly below average. These were only 18 percent occupied compared to 52 percent for the study at large.

The distance of a bat house to the nearest potential flight obstacles, usually tree branches, was significantly related to occupancy. Those less than five feet from obstacles were only 24 percent used, compared to 76 percent for those 20 feet or more from obstacles. As will be discussed, factors such as forest density, distance to nearest obstacles, and exposure to solar heating are not independent of one another.

Two bat houses mounted back-to-back with an additional roosting chamber in between creates space for more than 600 bats. The brown color, vent slots, and north-south orientation provide a maximum temperature gradient. The houses are mounted 15 feet high on poles to protect the bats from climbing predators and to increase solar exposure. The location—near water and in an area of known bat activity greatly enhances success. (Note that the tongue-and-groove lumber used on these houses gives them the appearance of having more vents.)

Effect of mounting substrate—Occupancy rates differed significantly among houses mounted on buildings, poles, or trees. Houses located on poles were 81 percent occupied and those on buildings were 73 percent used, while those placed on trees (whether isolated or in a forest) achieved only 34 percent success. Sixty percent of the sample was northern, 6 percent mid-latitude, and 34 percent southern. Mounting substrate and exposure to solar heating are closely related, and bats appeared not to be actually choosing a particular substrate, but rather exposure to sun.

Relevance of solar radiation to dense forest, obstacles, and mounting substrate—Looking at the data showing highest occupancy rates on poles and least in dense forest, we hypothesized that exposure to sun might explain these differences. Indeed, houses mounted on poles received an average of nine hours of daily sun, compared to seven for those mounted on buildings and only two hours on trees. Furthermore, it was found that nearby obstacles, usually tree branches, significantly reduced the amount of sun reaching houses.

To test our hypothesis, we predicted that if reduced solar heating were the primary determinant of low use rates for houses on trees, tree-mounted houses receiving more than four hours of daily sun would have use rates comparable to those mounted on buildings or poles. Knowing that bat needs for solar warming may differ between northern and southern localities, this test was limited to houses located at latitudes north of 40 degrees.

Northern houses mounted on trees, but still receiving four or more hours of sun daily, were significantly more likely to be occupied than those receiving less. In fact, such houses achieved occupancy rates of 82 percent, compared to 81 percent for poles and 73 percent for buildings. It seems clear that the mounting substrate is not as important as hours of exposure to sun.

Assuming too little sun to be the reason for poor occupancy rates on trees, it was postulated that houses on southern trees should be better used than their northern counterparts. Indeed, occupancy rates for houses on southern trees proved to be significantly higher than for those on northern trees. The 17 percent improvement likely would have been even greater except that little brown bats are uncommon in the South, while Mexican free-tailed bats are among the most frequent users of southern houses. Free-tails are high-speed flyers that may not choose to risk flying into the increased obstacles around many tree-mounted houses. Thus far, their only known use has been limited to houses mounted on buildings or poles.

Answers to Common Bat House Questions

Will attracting bats to bat houses in my yard increase the likelihood that they will move into my attic or wall spaces?
No. If bats liked your attic or wall spaces, they probably would already be living there.

If I have bats living in my attic, but would prefer that they occupy a bat house instead, what should I do?
Attics and other parts of buildings often provide ideal bat roosting sites. This is especially true for nursery colonies, which prefer stable high temperatures and the ability to move up and down to select from a range of available temperatures under varied weather conditions. Sometimes an attic is only marginally suited to bat needs, and a good bat house large enough to shelter the whole colony may tempt them to move without other encouragement. This is especially true when a group of several houses ensures a range of available temperatures at a nearby location.

In most cases, however, bats will not voluntarily move from an attic. In such cases, alternative roosts ideally should be provided several weeks or months before the desired move. The bats should be evicted from the attic at a time in early spring or late summer when flightless young are not present.

Eviction is often easily accomplished. Watch to see where the bats emerge at dusk. Then cut a piece of polypropylene bird netting (available at yard and garden stores) large enough to hang over the emergence point, extending at least a foot below and to each side of each exit. Tape it in place so that it hangs free an inch or two from the building at the bottom. It will then serve as a one-way valve, permitting emergence, but closing when bats land on it to return. There are many documented cases of successful relocations to bat houses that have been carried out in this manner.

Can bats be introduced into areas where they do not already live?
If appropriate bat species pass through your general area, you may, by putting up a bat house, attract a colony, but there is nothing you can do to introduce them artificially. They have strong homing instincts and likely would return to their original roost. Thus, catching or purchasing bats (which is illegal) for introduction into a new bat house should not be attempted.

How can I determine the likelihood of attracting bats?
Most North American bats prefer to live within a few

Many people who have bats in their attic, and who erected a bat house before they made repairs to evict the bats, have been successful in persuading the bats to move into the alternate roost. Putting up bird netting over the bats' entry holes allows them to leave but not to return.

hundred yards of water, especially streams, rivers, or lakes. However, some bat houses up to two miles from water have attracted bachelor colonies. In some western areas, even small cattle tanks that provide open water may be sufficient. All bats, especially nursery colonies, require good feeding habitat; riparian areas are typically best. Exceptionally high bat house success has been achieved in areas that support a mixture of varied agriculture, especially orchards and natural woodlots or other vegetation near water. Areas where bats already have attempted to live in buildings are a good bet, and the nearer they are to potential hibernating sites in caves or abandoned mines the better.

Why might bats not be attracted to my bat house?
It may not be well built, most frequently meaning failure to: 1) provide 3/4-inch-wide roosting crevices that are at least 15 inches deep; 2) carefully caulk and paint; or 3) include ventilation slots. Also, even well-built houses must be positioned and painted an appropriate shade of color to provide adequate solar heating, and they should be as safe as possible from climbing predators.

If your bat house meets construction, mounting, and habitat criteria and still has not attracted bats by the end of its second full spring-summer season of avail-

With their voracious appetite for beetles, bugs, and leafhoppers, big brown bats are among a farmer's best allies in reducing agricultural pests.

ability, try moving it to a location with more or less sun. Many bat house owners have achieved dramatically improved success by simply moving their houses, typically to receive more sun.

Some areas simply do not provide bats with adequate food, water, or hibernation sites. These areas will not support bats in buildings either.

Alternatively, in a few places, bats may simply have all the roosts they need and are unlikely to move until they lose an existing roost or until you provide a better home than they already have. This is where patient testing comes into play! So far, we are unaware of any large areas in North America (with the possible exception of some unusually hot desert lowlands) where bats have not been attracted.

How effective are bats in controlling insects?
As primary predators of night-flying insects, bats play a key role in the balance of nature. They consume vast quantities of insects, including many agricultural and yard pests. Little brown bats often feed on mosquitoes when they are abundant, and just one bat can catch hundreds in a single hour. They also are excellent predators of moths, which produce such costly pests as cutworms, corn earworms, and army worms. Organic farmer Tony Koch reports a reduction of corn earworms from an average of several per ear of corn to

none since he successfully attracted approximately 2,000 little brown bats that live in 21 bat houses on his Oregon farm. Many pests avoid areas where they hear bats.

Bat biologist Dr. John Whitaker recently documented that a single colony of 150 big brown bats, a number that could easily live in one bat house, can eliminate 38,000 cucumber beetles, 16,000 June bugs, 19,000 stink bugs, and 50,000 leafhoppers in a summer. This is a conservative number that does not consider the many other unidentified insects these bats eat. Cucumber beetles are among America's most costly agricultural pests. Adults attack corn, spinach, and various vine plants, but the greatest harm comes from their larvae, known as corn rootworms. Whitaker concluded that by eating 38,000 cucumber beetles, the bats protected local farmers from approximately 18 million rootworms that the beetles would have produced.

Illustrative of the incredible impact bats can have, the 20 million Mexican free-tailed bats living in Bracken Cave, Texas, consume up to 250 tons of insects in a single night over surrounding towns and croplands. Loss of such bats leaves us increasingly dependent on toxic chemical alternatives that already seriously threaten our personal and environmental health.

Will having bat houses in my yard interfere with attracting birds?
No. They will not compete, either for food or space.

Will bat droppings pose a health threat to my family?
No more so than bird or cat droppings would. Inhalation of dust associated with animal feces of any kind should be avoided.

What are the odds that a sick bat will endanger my family with rabies?
Like all mammals, bats can contract rabies, though very few (less than half of one percent) do. Unlike many other animals, even rabid bats rarely become aggressive. They quickly die from the disease, and outbreaks in their colonies are extremely rare. The odds of being harmed by a rabid bat are remote if you simply do not attempt to handle bats. Any bat that appears easy to catch should be assumed sick and left alone.

Fewer than 25 Americans are believed to have contracted rabies from bats in the past five decades. Nearly as many people die annually from contact with household pets. With or without bats in your yard, the most important action you can take to protect your family from rabies is to vaccinate your family dogs and cats.

Bats Most Likely to Occupy Bat Houses

THROUGHOUT THE NORTHERN two-thirds of the United States and southern Canada, the little brown bat and the big brown bat are the most likely species to be encountered in bat houses. In the south, Mexican free-tailed and evening bats are the most common. In general, any species that naturally roosts in buildings or under bridges is a candidate for a bat house. The following species are confirmed or suspected bat house users. Several additional species likely will be found using bat houses.

Pallid bat, *Antrozous pallidus*
WESTERN AND SOUTHWESTERN U.S., mostly in arid areas. Found in rock crevices, buildings, under bridges, and in bat houses. Winter habitat unknown, presumed to hibernate locally in deep rock crevices.

Big brown bat, *Eptesicus fuscus*
MOST OF THE U.S. and Canada, except for extreme southern Florida. Rears young in tree hollows and buildings. Hibernates in caves, abandoned mines, and buildings. Frequent bat house users that have also overwintered in bat houses from Texas to New York.

Southeastern bat, *Myotis austroriparius*
MOSTLY RESTRICTED to Gulf States. Rears young in caves, tree hollows, and buildings. Mostly non-migratory, hibernates in caves in northern range and often in tree hollows or buildings farther south. Believed to use bat houses in the Gulf States.

Little brown bat, *Myotis lucifugus*
WOODED AREAS throughout most of Canada and the northern half of the U.S., except desert and arid areas. A few isolated populations farther south. Rears young in tree hollows, buildings, rock crevices, and bat houses. Travels to nearest suitable cave or abandoned mine for hibernation. This is the species that most commonly occupies bat houses.

Eastern long-eared bat, *Myotis septentrionalis*
UPPER MIDWEST and East into Canada, also ranging south into northern Arkansas, Tennessee, western Alabama, and eastern Georgia. Summer roosts are varied, and these bats have been found beneath tree bark, in buildings, and at night in caves. Little is known about their nursery colonies, but small numbers have been found rearing young beneath tree bark, in buildings, and in bat houses. Hibernates in rock crevices, caves, and mines.

Cave myotis, *Myotis velifer*
SOUTHERN ARIZONA and New Mexico into West Texas and Oklahoma, and extreme south-central Kansas. Forms large nursery colonies in caves. Also rears young in smaller groups in buildings, often in crevices. The eastern subspecies hibernates in caves, but the winter habitat of the western subspecies is unknown. Shares bat houses with Mexican free-tailed bats in Texas.

Yuma myotis, *Myotis yumanensis*
ALL OF WESTERN Canada, Washington, Idaho, Oregon, California, Arizona, extreme western Nevada, eastern Utah, southern Colorado to western New Mexico. Restricted to areas near water. Rears young in caves, in buildings, and under bridges. Winter habitat unknown. Lives in bat houses from Arizona to southwestern Canada.

Evening bat, *Nycticeius humeralis*
EAST OF THE Appalachians, ranges from southern Pennsylvania to Florida. West of these mountains, it occurs from extreme southern Michigan and Wisconsin, west to southeastern Nebraska, and south through eastern and southern Texas. Abundant in southern coastal states. Rears young in buildings, tree cavities, and bat houses. Forms nursery colonies numbering in the hundreds, often sharing roosts with Mexican free-tailed bats. Winter habitat unknown.

Eastern pipistrelle, *Pipistrellus subflavus*
EASTERN NORTH AMERICA into Canada, except northern New England. Most of the Midwest, except Michigan, northern Indiana, and western Wisconsin. South from eastern Minnesota to eastern Texas and central Florida. Abundant over much of the Southeast. Little known about summer roosts; sometimes rears young in buildings. Several pipistrelles twice reported in bat houses. Hibernates in caves.

Mexican free-tailed bat, *Tadarida brasiliensis*
COMMON IN southern and southwestern U.S., and north to Nebraska, Colorado, Utah, Nevada, and Oregon. Rears young in caves, in buildings, under bridges, and in bat houses. A frequent bat house user. Migrates to overwinter in caves of Mexico and Central America. Non-migratory in Florida. Remains active year-round.

PHOTOS BY MERLIN D. TUTTLE

For further information:
If you are interested in learning more about bats, particularly those that might occupy your bat house, Merlin Tuttle's book, *America's Neighborhood Bats*, can help. Numerous color photographs and identification keys will assist you in understanding and identifying the most common American bats. It is available at bookstores or through BCI's free catalogue.